GLASTONBURY ABBEY

THE ISLE OF AVALON

a Christian sanctuary
so ancient that only legend
can record its origin

A Pitkin Guide

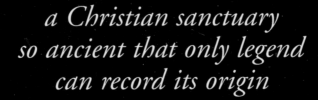

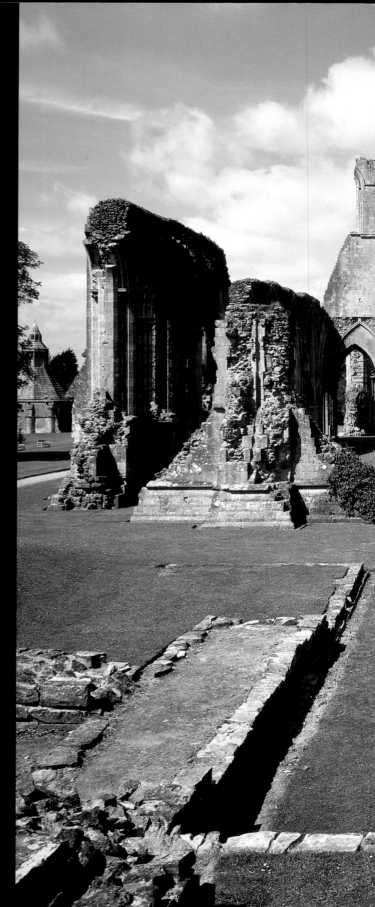

The ruins of Glastonbury Abbey, set among noble trees and well kept lawns, are all that remain today of one of the greatest monasteries of medieval England. When the abbey was dissolved in 1539 the buildings were stripped and the walls left to the neglect of 350 years. Much of the town is built of stone from the ruins.

A Unique Two Thousand Years of History

1st century:
Foundation of the Old Church of St Mary.

***c.*720:**
Saxon stone church built.

940–956:
Abbacy of St Dunstan. Expansion of extent and wealth of church and monastery.

1184:
Church and monastery destroyed by fire.

1189:
Lady Chapel consecrated.

1213:
Great Church consecrated.

1539:
Dissolution of the abbey. Abbot Whiting and two monks executed on Glastonbury Tor.

1907:
Ruins purchased by the Church of England.

GLASTONBURY ABBEY
THE ISLE OF AVALON

The Legends of Avalon

Back in the mists of antiquity, the Glastonbury area was a focus of mythology. Many and fantastic are the stories of Avalon, a body of legends still alive and growing today. The unique 150-metre landmark of Glastonbury Tor, rising sheer from the Somerset Levels, seems to be the inspiration behind it all. This fine eminence can be seen from many miles away, yet is invisible from certain angles very nearby. Was there a maze here, a centre for fertility rites to the great earth goddess? Is this 'isle of glass' a centre for ley-lines, routes of spiritual energy which are said to link prehistoric and religious sites?

Two thousand years ago, the sea washed right to the foot of Glastonbury Tor, being succeeded gradually by a vast lake. In the 3rd century BC the Celts founded a lake village nearby, and it is in Celtic legend that the name Avalon has its origin from the demi-god Avalloc or Avallach who ruled the underworld. Ancient lore has it that Avalon, where sea met land, was the meeting place of the dead, where they passed to another level of existence.

However much or little one believes in the mythology that is so much a part of the fabric of Glastonbury, there is no doubt that the district has an atmosphere all its own. The visitor does not have to linger long in this place to become aware of a deep interest and involvement with spiritual values, the natural legacy of the striving of ancient man in this area to come to terms with the forces of earth and sky.

RIGHT: *Glastonbury Tor and St Michael's Chapel. For many centuries the Tor has been the subject of myths and legends. In later centuries it has been a Christian focus, and an almost obligatory part of any pilgrimage to Glastonbury, both in medieval times and today.* **J**

INSET: *The ruins of the abbey lend themselves to many unexpected and dramatic views. Each season brings new surprises.* **8**

The Transition to Christianity

How did the isolated Isle of Avalon become the site of one of the greatest monasteries in Britain? Tales of a miraculous cauldron or grail form a very strong thread through Celtic mythology. It appears that over time this concept of a special vessel – a source and symbol of spiritual nourishment – became interwoven with Christ and the Last Supper. Legend has it that Joseph of Arimathea, who placed Christ's body in the tomb, obtained the Holy Grail as a memento of Christ. After many years he brought it to Glastonbury, burying it near the Tor on Chalice Hill, perhaps by Chalice Well, the principal spring on the island. A great pagan Celtic sanctuary is thought to have grown up here, its focus most likely being the well. The existence of this sanctuary would explain the coming of the earliest missionaries.

Today, the Tor is crowned by the 14th-century Chapel of St Michael, but this is probably the successor to many shrines, Christian and pre-Christian, which have faced the elements on this hill.

ABOVE: *Joseph of Arimathea; a window in St John's Church. Legend has it that Joseph, the man who took charge of Christ's body after the Crucifixion, visited Glastonbury with the boy Jesus. He is said to have built the original wattle church on the site where Glastonbury Abbey later stood.* (E)

LEFT: *The site of the Glastonbury thorn on Wearyall Hill. According to local legend, Joseph of Arimathea and his 12 companions arrived by boat at the hill. Joseph stuck his staff in the ground and it took root.* (H)

We know that a chapel stood on the hill before 1275, when it was thrown down in an earthquake. Once the old high place was sanctified by the erection of a Christian chapel, the missionaries might well have chosen to settle in the more sheltered and convenient site where the abbey later rose. The Somerset tradition surrounding Joseph is that he and the boy Jesus built Glastonbury's first church. More credible sources indicate that the church was founded by missionaries who accompanied King Lucius, an early British ruler, back to Glastonbury from Rome in the 2nd century. They converted the local inhabitants and built a church on the site of the present Lady Chapel. It was simply constructed, of wattle and daub: interwoven branches packed with clay, muck etc, applied by hand.

The church was dedicated to the Virgin Mary, and Glastonbury became the first home (*c.*500) of the Marian cult in Britain. The grail became Mary's emblem. Indeed, the title 'Our Lady St Mary of Glastonbury' has survived to this day.

ABOVE: *Chalice Well at the foot of Tor Hill. Set in a delightful garden, it is fed by a nearby spring which delivers 25,000 gallons of water per day at a constant temperature of 52°F. Frederick Bligh Bond, designer of the symbolic well cover, and the abbey's first Director of Excavations, was dismissed in 1922 for his interest in psychic phenomena.* Ⓖ

TOP RIGHT: *The Chapel of St Michael which stands at the top of Glastonbury Tor.* Ⓙ

RIGHT: *An artist's impression of Glaston, the first Christian settlement of AD 37, with its wattle church at the centre.*

King Arthur

The core of Glastonbury's first monastery was the ancient cemetery which had grown around the old church of St Mary, to the south of where the Lady Chapel stands today. Very early graves are packed together here – an eager attempt by the great men of the neighbourhood to obtain burial as near as possible to the oratories and tombs of the saints which studded the area.

One of these graves is believed to have been that of King Arthur, perhaps the greatest figure of medieval romance, a person who almost certainly existed but whose career is surrounded by legend. Glastonbury has traditionally been associated with Arthur. An early legend has it that his wife, Guinevere, was kidnapped by Melwas, king of Summer Land (Somerset), imprisoned in his castle on the Tor and rescued by the bold Arthur who rode with his army from the far south-west. From this, it was perhaps inevitable that the story of King Arthur and his Knights of the Round Table should have become interwoven with the quest for the Holy Grail.

Even when stripped of the trappings of mythology, there clearly did exist a Celtic prince or warlord who succeeded in halting the pagan Saxon advance across the land. It is also confirmed that the monks found a grave of Celtic origin in 1191. A few feet above the coffin, they found a leaden cross with a Latin inscription (inset right) which claimed that the body was that of King Arthur. Whether this is true or not was not an issue of the day, and in 1278 the remains were ceremonially translated to a shrine in the choir of the Great Church of the new monastery. The proceedings were witnessed by King Edward I, who took a great interest in Arthurian legend.

When the monastery was dissolved in the 16th century, the shrine was despoiled, and Arthur's grave was lost amongst the rubble of the ruined church. It was only in 1934 that excavations revealed the final resting place of the king, a site marked with a humble plaque today.

INSET ABOVE RIGHT: *A 17th-century drawing made by William Camden of the cross which he claimed came from Arthur's grave.*

INSET BELOW RIGHT: *In 1191, monks claimed to have identified the remains of the 6th-century leader, King Arthur, and his consort Guinevere. These were entombed in a shrine in the choir in 1278, rediscovered in a 1934 excavation.*

OPPOSITE PAGE: *A 13th-century miniature by Matthew Paris of the coronation of King Arthur. It is likely that Paris would not have doubted Arthur's existence or his status as king.*

Saxons and Normans

In the 7th century Somerset was conquered by the Saxons, who by then were converts to Christianity. They re-endowed the monastery and their king, Ine of Wessex, erected a new principal church of stone at what is now the west end of the nave. This was enlarged once in the 8th century and again by St Dunstan who was Abbot of Glastonbury (940–56) and later Archbishop of Canterbury.

ABOVE: *Another artist's impression of the original wattle church on the site of the abbey. Comparison with the settlement picture on page 5 shows that its size and shape are by no means certain.*

Perhaps the most important figure in the abbey's history, Dunstan was born nearby, becoming Abbot at a time when both the fabric and the religious life of the abbey were at a very low ebb. His main work lay in the monastic buildings which he erected to the south of the church, the earliest example of the cloistered layout in England. Dunstan lengthened Ine's church, adding a tower and aisles. The result resembled the monastery at Cluny in Burgundy, and was truly a huge church. Little remains of it today.

Under Dunstan, Glastonbury's wealth increased. King Edgar showered the abbey with gifts of land and relics of gold and silver, and at the time of the Domesday Book, the abbey was the richest in England.

ABOVE: *St Dunstan, Abbot of Glastonbury 940–56; from a window in Street parish church. Dunstan was behind a spiritual and physical revival at Glastonbury, inspired by his exile in France.*

ABOVE: *The seal of St Mary's, Glastonbury, possibly 13th-century, or earlier. The dedication of the church to St Mary dates back at least to pre-Saxon times.*

The Norman conquest brought considerable strains to the abbey. The first Norman Abbot, Turstin, quarrelled with the Saxon monks and brought archers into the church to shoot those who dared to argue with his edicts. It is alleged that two monks died. Despite this he was, like many Normans, a builder. He thought the Saxon church unworthy and started a new one. This in turn was considered insufficient by Abbot Herlewin who, early in the 12th century, planned yet another, this time on a magnificent scale, copying the great church at St Albans of a generation earlier. The church was completed by Herlewin's successor, Henry of Blois, a brother of King Stephen and Bishop of Winchester, who also rebuilt the whole range of monastic buildings enclosing the cloister. The Norman churches were built east of the Lady Chapel or old church, which continued in existence. This removal was designed to preserve the ancient cemetery, still the sacred centre of the abbey.

On 25 May 1184 fire consumed the great monastery of Glastonbury and almost all the treasures within. Only one chamber and the bell tower were left standing. The rest of these new and wondrous buildings and the venerable church, the shelter of so many saints, hallowed as the first Christian church in Britain, were reduced to a heap of ashes.

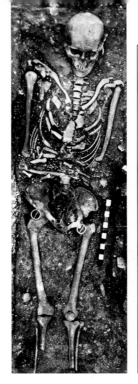

William of Malmesbury
(*c.*1090–*c.*1143)

ONE of the leading historians of his age, William studied the antiquities of the Church of Glastonbury using the records of the abbey. In doing this, William enjoyed the hospitality of the abbey and would have been loath to discredit cherished legends, although he did state his scepticism concerning the Joseph of Arimathea connection. He does however, record connections with a number of the greatest saints of the Celtic world, including St Patrick, the apostle of Ireland (*c.*389–461). Most of the records that William used perished in the great fire of 1184.

ABOVE: *The bones of Seffrid, Abbot of Glastonbury (c.1120–25) and Bishop of Chichester, who fell foul of King Stephen and was forced to retire to Glastonbury to live the life of a simple monk. The bones were revealed in Radford's excavations of the 1960s.*

BELOW: *St Patrick's Chapel dates from the abbacy of Richard Beere. It contains a drinking vessel for holy water and a stone altar. Beside it is one of the holy thorn trees.*

The Abbey Reborn

The destruction of the monastic buildings in the fire of 1184 posed many questions, administrative and financial. The first need was to find a place where the services of the church could be continued. Excavations have shown that the ruined 12th-century nave was patched up and served for nearly 30 years, until the eastern part of the new church was ready.

The financial problem was initially solved by royal generosity, which enabled an immediate start to be made on the rebuilding. King Henry II regularly supplied funds to support the work when local income proved insufficient. His successor Richard I, his mind on overseas matters, proved less generous.

The first building erected was the existing Lady Chapel, which was completed and dedicated within a few years of the fire. It owed its unusual position at the west of the church to the fact that it replaced the old church of St Mary, the most venerable of the destroyed shrines.

The chapel is in the fully developed Romanesque style of the late 12th century. It is entirely cased in a fine ashlar of stone from Doulting in the nearby Mendip Hills, with some dressings and details in the local blue lias, giving it a rich polychrome effect.

Internally the lower stage is adorned with an interlacing arcade while above, the chapel was lighted by large windows with fine carved detail. The stonework above the doors is elaborately sculptured with concentric rows of small figure scenes.

The proportions of the building are now marred by the crypt, inserted about 1500 by Abbot Beere. This necessitated the raising of the original floor level. The vaulting of the crypt has fallen except at the east end where it extends under the western bay of the Galilee, or porch, linking the Lady Chapel with the Great Church to the east. On the south side of the crypt is a recess which covers a well; its elaborate niche is ornamented identically to the chapel's windows. This is clearly a well of special importance, probably dating from the early days of the abbey. The chapel's history is lost, as the original name was replaced by that of Joseph of Arimathea, whose cult was developed by Abbot Beere and localized in the crypt.

LEFT: *The west window and the head of the arcade in the lower stage illustrate the beauty of the Lady Chapel. The tracery in the windows is part of the restoration carried out by Abbot Beere at the turn of the 16th century.* ②

RIGHT: *The fine Romanesque north door of the Lady Chapel, richly ornamented with foliage and figure scenes.* ②

BELOW: *The beautiful south side of the Lady Chapel with wide expanses of fine ashlar masonry, enriched with ornamental geometrical patterns with foliage and tendrils.* ②

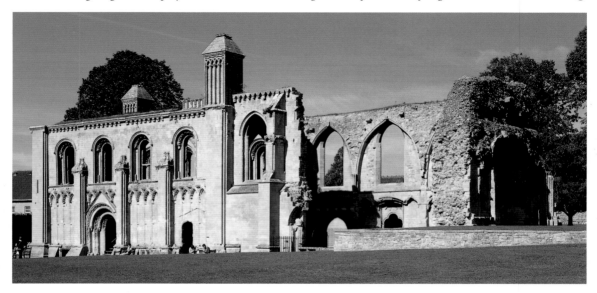

The Great Church Grows

The Great Church, begun late in the 12th century, was sufficiently advanced for the monks to take possession on Christmas Day 1213. This does not necessarily mean that the building was anywhere near complete. It is likely that at that time only the walls of the eastern part, including the crossing, were up, with temporary roofing to keep out the elements. The addition of a stone vault could be carried out later. The new eastern arm was of four bays with an ambulatory and a large projecting chapel of three bays at the back of the high altar. The transepts were regular with two chapels on each side. The inner chapel on the north side, dedicated in honour of St Thomas Becket, is well preserved and gives a good idea of their appearance. The north transept had a western aisle. It was in this aisle that the Loretto Chapel was later placed by Abbot Beere. The main elevation of the Great Church retained the traditional three stages, but the emphasis on the middle stage, or triforium, masking the pent roofs over the aisles, is considerably reduced. This stage and the arcade below are contained in a single giant order of arches. The detail is very fine and pure early

ABOVE: *The view from the choir across the south transept to the Abbot's kitchen. Before the dissolution and subsequent ruin of the abbey, the intervening area was occupied by the cloister of the monastery and beyond it the splendid Abbot's house, enlarged and rebuilt by Abbot de Breynton in the 14th century. Dominating this house, and adjoining the kitchen on its north-east corner, was the Abbot's hall.* ⑧

Gothic with well-jointed ashlar throwing into relief the scanty ornament. Originally the walls were intended for displaying paintings. The nave has been largely destroyed. Part of the south wall survives, showing no development in style from that of the eastern part of the church. This may not be significant as this wall was often built first in order to provide a backing for the cloister.

ABOVE: *The dogtooth carving of the arches is typically Romanesque in style.*

OPPOSITE PAGE: *The stark ruins at the former crossing of the Great Church.*

BELOW: *A model of the Great Church as it may have appeared in 1539, the year of its dissolution. The abbey was larger in its total area than Canterbury, and second in wealth only to Westminster. The model can be seen in the abbey museum.*

The Great Church Completed

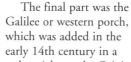

The west front of the Great Church was probably built in the first half of the 13th century with the flanking towers being added soon after 1250. This marked the completion of the main structure, but the furnishing and decoration of the Great Church continued for many years, the vaulting and painting of the nave being carried out only during the abbacy of Abbot Adam of Sodbury (1323–34).

The final part was the Galilee or western porch, which was added in the early 14th century in a rather richer style. Originally the choir of monks sat in the eastern bays of the nave, with the eastern arm containing the altar and shrine. In the mid 14th century, the choir were moved into a lengthened eastern arm. The ambulatory was also moved east with a range of five small chapels against the new east wall engulfing the older projecting chapel. This was only replaced 150 years later, when Abbot Beere built the Edgar Chapel, which was designed to contain the monuments to Edgar and other Saxon kings whom the abbey claimed as its founders.

ABOVE: *Stonework from the Great Church, now to be found in the abbey museum. After the dissolution, the abbey was sold to the Duke of Somerset, protector of the realm for the young Edward VI (1547–53), who systematically sold off stone from the walls for local building.*

RIGHT: *Medieval tiles from the Great Church, now to be found in the abbey museum.*

LEFT: *The abbey ruins looking east from the west doorway. In the background is Abbey House, formerly home to various owners of the abbey, now a Church of England retreat house.* (4)

OPPOSITE PAGE: *The interior of the Lady Chapel, looking to the west doorway of the Great Church. At the foot of the steps is the Galilee, a large porch or vestibule. Below is the undercroft.* (2)

INSET RIGHT: *The vault under the Galilee, often the scene of services in summer. Around 1500, Abbot Beere established it as a shrine to St Joseph of Arimathea, a reflection of his fascination for the saint and his entrepreneurial skill. The Arthurian legend was enjoying a revival and pilgrims came in their thousands.* (3)

The Power of the Abbot

A s the head of the second wealthiest abbey in Britain (behind Westminster Abbey), the Abbot of Glastonbury lived in considerable splendour and wielded tremendous power. Most large abbeys had the right to hold their own private courts. The 15th-century Tribunal which still stands today in the High Street may have been the latest of the buildings to house the Abbot's court, perhaps on the site where these courts had been held from a very early period.

ABOVE: *The 14th-century abbey barn used to store the grain due to the abbey in tithe. It is now the Somerset Rural Life Museum.* Ⓕ

The medieval abbey was an economic unit with its manors and other possessions supplying much of the needs of the great community. The 14th-century tithe barn south of the abbey was the central storehouse, to which the surrounding estates brought their tithe, a tenth part of their annual grain production.

The principal surviving testimony to the wealth of the abbey is the kitchen, part of the magnificent Abbot's house begun by John de Breynton (1334–42). Of its great hall only the south-west angle remains standing. Even this fragment shows the remarkable splendour of the building, which extended over a large area and included a garden. Other great houses belonging to the abbey were built on estates throughout Somerset and elsewhere, one of the most notable being the manor farm at Meare, three miles to the west. The estate there took in Meare Pool, a lake of several square miles which was the abbey's chief source of fish for fast days.

LEFT: *The Tribunal, on the High Street, where the Abbot's courts were held. The upper front room was the court; below was the antechamber or waiting room.* Ⓓ

BELOW LEFT: *Detail of the 14th-century cope found at Othery parish church and now on display in the abbey museum.*

INSET RIGHT: *This fine stone impression of a past abbot of Glastonbury is now displayed in the abbey museum.*

OPPOSITE PAGE: *Growing luxury and wealth dictated the provision of a separate kitchen for the Abbot's house. Inset is the ceiling, where eight curved ribs meet to form the central air holes.* ⑲

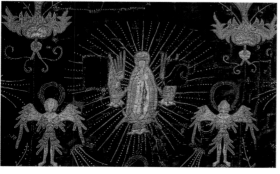

The Glastonbury Pilgrims

The Great Church of Glastonbury was a magnet which drew pilgrims not only from all over England but also from far beyond. They came to venerate the relics preserved in the abbey, the bones of saints and other objects of religious importance, placed in ornate shrines. Important visitors were normally accommodated within the abbey; excavations have disclosed a special apartment at the south end of the Abbot's house erected for the visit of King Henry II.

Outside the gates of the abbey, a small town serving its secular needs grew up in the course of centuries. The George and Pilgrims Hotel in the High Street, built in the 15th century, is thought to have housed more modest visitors. En route to the abbey, such a person would have made his way through the booths of many traders to enter the 14th-century main gate, which still survives. Inside the precincts a set route, marked by stations, would be followed. As part of their pilgrimage, many people would also climb the Tor to St Michael's Chapel. This marked what was probably the oldest sacred place in the area, rebuilt in the 14th and 15th centuries with the help of the offerings of pilgrims.

One of the stations where pilgrims paused to pray. It is situated on the south wall of the Lady Chapel and dates from the 13th century. ②

BELOW: *The George and Pilgrims Hotel, built in the late 15th century by Abbot John Selwood. Pilgrims who made offerings at the various shrines and altars were a valuable source of revenue to the monastery and they were accommodated according to their station. The most important patrons, notably royalty, would stay in the abbey. Henry VII, who came to Glastonbury in 1494, was lodged in a special apartment in the Abbot's house. Less illustrious but nonetheless wealthy patrons were housed in the purpose-built accommodation in the High Street pictured here.* Ⓒ

Dissolution and Decay

In 1536, the 27th year of the reign of Henry VIII, there were over 800 monasteries, nunneries and friaries in Britain. By 1541 there were none. Over 10,000 monks and nuns had been dispersed; the buildings had been seized by the Crown and sold off or leased to new lay occupiers. Glastonbury Abbey was one of the principal victims of this Dissolution of the Monasteries. Why did it happen?

Many religious houses were already in decline and in need of reform. Most were under-inhabited, particularly since the Black Death, and in many the quality of religious observance had diminished in inverse proportion to an over-indulgence in more worldly activities. It is also possible that the King feared the religious orders might work against his new independent Church of England. Yet the great majority of clerics, including Abbot Whiting of Glastonbury, had taken the oath upholding the Act of Supremacy without demur.

It would seem, though, that Henry's main motive for the dissolution was financial. Firstly, we know that his coffers were depleted. Secondly, all religious houses received the same treatment irrespective of their size and the quality of their religious observances.

The end of Glastonbury as a monastery was particularly brutal. In 1539, the gentle Whiting, now a frail old man, was found guilty of spurious offences, dragged up the Tor on a hurdle and executed with two of his monks. His head was struck off and placed on the abbey gateway, his body quartered and displayed in Bridgwater, Ilchester, Bath and Wells. The other 40 monks were driven out and any items of value in the abbey torn down and sold off to the highest bidder. Eventually, much of the stone found its way into buildings in the town and into the causeway to Wells which was being built at the time. Over the next 350 years, the site passed through many hands, becoming dilapidated and overgrown.

In 1907 the ruins were bought for £30,000 on behalf of the Church of England. Over the next 15 years, the undergrowth was cleared and the walls stripped of vegetation and cleaned. This means that the ruins of Glastonbury Abbey are now preserved for a new generation of pilgrims to visit.

BELOW: The abbey ruins from the south. The cloister and the ranges have been reduced to ground level and in most places only the lines of the walls are marked on the surface. (16)

RIGHT: A view of the Tor and the town from the air.

A portrait in stained glass of the ill-fated Abbot Whiting, who in 1539, by order of King Henry VIII, was dragged up the Tor and summarily executed with two of his monks.

The Modern Pilgrims

Glastonbury's Great Church may now be an impressive ruin, but the spiritual power that brought it into being lives on. The abbey is very much a living Christian sanctuary; many people visit with organized groups on mini-pilgrimages, and every Tuesday services are held in the undercroft or in St Patrick's Chapel.

The high point of the calendar is the weekend of the Glastonbury pilgrimages. These commence on the first Saturday in July. Started as a private event in 1924 by a few churches in the county, the pilgrimages have grown into a huge public expression of faith. People arrive in parties from a 150-mile radius, and individually from much further afield. The Anglican pilgrimage on the Saturday involves some 3,000 people and continues from dawn to dusk. The noon Eucharist in the ruined nave sees the congregation receive the sacrament from the presiding bishop and the many priests and deacons who help him. A Greek orthodox service is held in the undercroft to venerate the icon of Our Lady of Glastonbury.

In the afternoon, after being entertained by musicians, choirs and theatrical groups, today's pilgrims gather near St John's Church to process with their banners down the High Street and into the abbey ruins for Evensong.

The Roman Catholic pilgrimage on the Sunday afternoon starts on the slopes of the Tor, from where the Bishop of Clifton and a visiting dignitary lead singing pilgrims down to the ruins. Here High Mass is celebrated. Both pilgrimages aim to provide Christians (and those on the fringes of Christianity) with an enjoyable day out and the chance to renew their faith in the company of an army of fellow Christians. They are thus made aware, far more than in their weekly parish worship, of the scale and greatness of the Christian movement.